C000130069

797,885 Books

are available to read at

www.ForgottenBooks.com

Forgotten Books' App
Available for mobile, tablet & eReader

ISBN 978-1-333-34738-3
PIBN 10493564

This book is a reproduction of an important historical work. Forgotten Books uses
state-of-the-art technology to digitally reconstruct the work, preserving the original format
whilst repairing imperfections present in the aged copy. In rare cases, an imperfection in
the original, such as a blemish or missing page, may be replicated in our edition. We do,
however, repair the vast majority of imperfections successfully; any imperfections that
remain are intentionally left to preserve the state of such historical works.

Forgotten Books is a registered trademark of FB &c Ltd.
Copyright © 2015 FB &c Ltd.
FB &c Ltd, Dalton House, 60 Windsor Avenue, London, SW19 2RR.
Company number 08720141. Registered in England and Wales.

For support please visit www.forgottenbooks.com

1 MONTH OF
FREE
READING

at
www.ForgottenBooks.com

By purchasing this book you are
eligible for one month membership to
ForgottenBooks.com, giving you
unlimited access to our entire
collection of over 700,000 titles via
our web site and mobile apps.

To claim your free month visit:

www.forgottenbooks.com/free493564

* Offer is valid for 45 days from date of purchase. Terms and conditions apply.

English
Français
Deutsche
Italiano
Español
Português

www.forgottenbooks.com

Mythology Photography **Fiction**
Fishing Christianity **Art** Cooking
Essays Buddhism Freemasonry
Medicine **Biology** Music **Ancient**
Egypt Evolution Carpentry Physics
Dance Geology **Mathematics** Fitness
Shakespeare **Folklore** Yoga Marketing
Confidence Immortality Biographies
Poetry **Psychology** Witchcraft
Electronics Chemistry History **Law**
Accounting **Philosophy** Anthropology
Alchemy Drama Quantum Mechanics
Atheism Sexual Health **Ancient History**
Entrepreneurship Languages Sport
Paleontology Needlework Islam
Metaphysics Investment Archaeology
Parenting Statistics Criminology
Motivational

Complimentary Banquet

. , . TO . . .

MR. FREDERICK N. MARTINEZ,

**On his return from South and Central America
and the West Indies,**

Hotél Cecil (Medici Room), Tuesday, Nov. 8th, 1898.

UC SOUTHERN REGIONAL LIBRARY FACILITY

AA 000 959 270 0

AN illustrated account of the proceedings, speeches by well-known Members of Parliament and prominent commercial men, with press notices of interest on commercial matters generally. ✢ ✢ ✢ ✢ ✢ ✢ ✢ ✢ ✢

COMMITTEE OF BANQUET:

Ex-Sheriff THOMAS R. DEWAR, Esq., J.P., D.L., Chairman.

EUGENE ALBERGA, Esq.   JOHN L. GROSSMITH, Esq.
W. H. BURGESS, Esq.   G. HAROLD KENT, Esq.

SRLF
oct 5276

... Introduction ...

I HAVE much pleasure in presenting this brochure to my many friends both at home and abroad, giving an account of a Banquet in my honour at the Hotel Cecil, London, November 8th, 1898, by the Heads of the many Houses I have the honour of representing, on my return from a fourth tour through South and Central America and the West Indies.

I hope that in these few pages will be found sufficient interesting matter, so that my friends may spend a few moments to read its contents. I take this opportunity of thanking the Chiefs of my Houses for the signal honour conferred upon me, and I gladly avail myself through this medium of returning my most hearty thanks to the various Houses abroad, who have supported me, and with whom I have had the pleasure of doing very agreeable business.

FREDERICK N. MARTINEZ.

London,
  January, 1899.

3021478

Complimentary Banquet

·· TO ·

MR. FREDERICK N MARTINEZ,

On his return from South and Central America and the West Indies,

HELD ON THE

8TH NOVEMBER, AT THE HOTEL CECIL,

Under the Presidency of Ex=Sheriff T. R. DEWAR, J.P., D.L.

Vice=President, GEORGE HAROLD KENT, Esq.

THE CHAIRMAN, in proposing the toast of "The Queen and Royal Family," said: Gentlemen, in a company of such busy and practical men I know it is usual that we should start the elocution of the evening in drinking that toast which is invariably the rule when true Britishers are gathered together : continued good health and long life to our Most Gracious Majesty the Queen. I am sure you will appreciate to-night the remark that commerce follows the flag, seeing that we are gathered together this evening to do honour to one of the Ambassadors of Commerce, of British Industries, in our good friend Mr. Martinez (hear, hear), and I am sure that you will say that it is the earnest desire of all true Englishmen that Her Majesty may be long spared to live, and to rule over that ever increaving Empire of which we are all so proud. Gentlemen, I give you the health of Her Majesty the Queen.

THE CHAIRMAN, in proposing the "Guest of the Evening," said: Gentlemen, I now claim your attention for a few moments. You have, no doubt, seen a few empty chairs to-night, but I do not think the absentees amount to the usual average. I have been told by a caterer that he generally counted on ten per cent. of the audience not turning up, so I think we are well within the limit, and they have all sent very good explanations of absence. For instance, we have a wire here from Madrid from one of the principals of the firms that Mr. Martinez represents. He says: "Only just received notice of banquet. Sorry. Impossible to be present. Have cabled to be represented. 'Mi curazon con Ud.'"—which is not pretty to those who are not acquainted with the Spanish language, but I am credibly informed that the translation is "My heart is with you." The telegram is signed "Gordon," of the firm of Gordon Ramirez & Co. We have also a message from a locality just as well known, where they sometimes fight naval engagements and have fierce encounters by land, and that is from Fleet Street. It reads: "Tell Chairman and Martinez how profoundly sorry I am that I cannot join you to-night. Ross, Editor *Black and White.*" And we also all regret the absence for the moment of that very distinguished politician, Mr. T. P O'Connor. Mr. O'Connor, M.P., writes to Mr. Martinez: "I am afraid I shall not be able to be at the dinner as I am suffering from dyspepsia at this moment, and a dinner always means a bad night; but I will turn up after dinner and take part in the pleasant gathering in your honour. Yours truly, T. P. O'Connor." We have also had letters from Mr. Bartholomew, of Bryant & May, and from Mr. Lumley, of L. Lumley & Co. Now we all deeply regret the absence of these gentlemen, and it is only very pressing engagements, and in some cases indisposition, that has kept them absent this evening. It is now my privilege to ask you to drink to the toast of the evening: "Our Guest." Now little did I think that we should have had the Press with us to-night, or I should have had an elaborate preparation (laughter), because I feel myself in the position of Sir Robert Walpole, when the Members of Parliament attempted to suppress the Press reports. He knocked the whole scheme on the head when he said to them : "Gentlemen, you forget that the Press make better speeches for us than we do ourselves." (Laughter.) Now I will trust to the good offices of the gentlemen of the Press that they will insert, in any copy that they may be pleased to give me, some of their own impressions if possible. because I can assure you when I have the honour of getting a small editorial in the newspapers of what I had said the previous evening, upon my word I could not possibly remember having used that language. (Laughter.) We all know our Mr. Martinez. (Hear, hear.) I say "our" advisedly, because we claim him as ours. We should not be here to-night in the force we are had we not had the privilege of saying that he is our Ambassador of Commerce. This is a unique gathering for a unique man (hear, hear), because I consider that any gentleman who represents such a list of firms as he does at the present moment, with a halo (here the Chairman held up the illustrated menu), if you turn them upside down—it may be egotistical for us to say so—names that we are proud enough to believe and to hope are second to none in our particular line of calling in this United Kingdom. (Hear, hear.) This, gentlemen, is a great production. There has been considerable conception in this menu. You will observe on the back that you get a biographical sketch of our friend Mr. Martinez. You get Mr. Martinez at home and abroad ; you know that Mr. Martinez's birthplace was in St. Thomas, West Indies, and I think you will agree with me that this place might be included in the same category as Scotland sometimes is, that is, " a grand place to emigrate from." Well, I need not tell you that Mr. Martinez did emigrate from this—what shall I call it—desert in the wilderness, and it was his intention no doubt to go one better, but to my mind he did not go much better, because he went to Panama. Now Panama is noted for—I do not know what you would call it—a big swindle, but I have heard it associated with what has not been very creditable in the way of bankruptcies ; but we are getting a few of them ourselves. And I am sure, although the gentlemen of the Press may think it very cheap copy in the dull season, especially what with that and the gentlemen coming from desert islands near Australia and other parts, I often think myself of discarding my own down-trodden trade and coming to Fleet Street. Mr. Martinez must have been reared in some extraordinary way like Romulus and Remus, because he has developed into the extraordinary individuality that he is. At twenty-six years of age—you may doubt my word, but we have got Mr. Martinez, Senior, here—he represents over twenty very respectable high class firms. (Laughter.) Now after this banquet it is not the intention that we should lose our Mr. Martinez, and if there should be any enterprising, energetic company promoter present who will issue a prospectus to-morrow morning—" Martinez Limited or Unlimited "—I trust that that gentleman will give us the first offer of shares, and being associated with that Company I think that we can assure that promoter that there will be no disclaimers the morning after. We have to thank Mr. Martinez for the extraordinary way he has represented us one and all, and I think the assurance of every principal here, and the principals of the individual firms are many (and I observe that if the principal is not here he is represented by the moving spirit of the concern) ; and these principals have come around you this evening, Mr. Martinez, to do honour to you, and they assure me that they are all glad to welcome you back from those countries famous for yellow-jack, typhoid and diphtheria, after you have pioneered

Mr. Martinez being Entertained at the Hotel Cecil, November 8th, 1898,
By the Chiefs of the Houses he Represents in South and Central America and the West Indies.

round that continent of South America and those unhappy islands in the West Indies, and have planted their names in the uttermost ends of the earth. We appreciate all those newspaper reports and all those sketches which you were good enough to send us at all times from the unearthly places to which you got. We consider, however, that there is an English word that is often misplaced, and that is "indefatigable"; but there is no one round this table to-night who will say that that word is not placed in the correct way when we say that you are an indefatigable and an irresistible Ambassador of Commerce. (Hear, hear.) Well, the whole of us round this table can remember the time when we entered into an understanding with Mr. Martinez, and the marvellous thing is how he has collected together in only three years such a *clientèle* of firms to represent, and I will give you one example of my own experience, and I know of one or two others. Mr. Martinez entered my office and said that a friend had told him to go round to us, and that he wanted to represent us; that he was going to Spain and wanted samples and cards. I said, "Well, stop a minute, let us talk about this." He simply answered, "I know I can represent you." These are the irresistible manners with which he approaches a man in his own den, and within two days he was away with my samples. And yet another case. Our honoured Vice-President informed me —and we had a good laugh over it—that Mr. Martinez introduced himself on a railway platform, and said to him, "I am going to represent your firm," and he did so within a fortnight's time and went to the West Indies. Now if a representative can approach a firm in that way, how can he approach clients abroad? I venture to believe that Mr. Martinez is beginning a career which will surprise us all (hear, hear), and in saying that I will say that it is our wish that Mr. Martinez should live long, and that he should represent us in the future as he has done in the past. We shall get jealous if we see many more coming on the list, but I trust that he will go forth in his future undertakings, and that he will satisfy us to the very highest and most sanguine of our ideals. I must ask you to drink to the long life and further prosperity of Mr. Frederick N. Martinez. (Cheers.)

("For he's a jolly good fellow" was then sung. and the health of Mrs. Martinez and family was drunk with enthusiasm.)

MR. F. N. MARTINEZ said : Mr. Chairman and Gentlemen, in coming before you as a public speaker, I must crave your kind indulgence. I think this is the first time I have had the honour of rising to speak before such distinguished gentlemen. I am more than flattered and perhaps a little bit bashful. I have to thank Mr. Dewar for his very kind remarks about me to-night, which I from my heart fully appreciate, and I thank you gentlemen all for so kindly and cordially receiving his remarks, and for toasting my health. Before forgetting it I have to thank you very kindly for mentioning the name of my good wife and family. It is a great pleasure and honour to me to be invited to dine with you this evening. I can assure you that it repays me more for the services which I have rendered you than if you had presented me with a fine coronet. I am afraid that my words will not adequately express to you how deeply I feel this favour, and especially as Mr. Dewar has done me the honour of taking the Chair this evening. I can assure you that he has been a very good friend to me, and a generous and kind master. I do not take upon myself entirely the honour you have done me this evening. I take it as an honour to my brothers in arms, to all other commercial travellers over the world from north to south, and from east to west. I am afraid that you have accorded this honour to one of its very poorest members. (No, no.) Well, I have done my duty for you, you have paid me, and you have done still more; you have honoured me to-night by inviting me to dine with you, and I can assure you that I feel the honour very greatly. I suppose that on looking at the menu to-night, to which our exalted Chairman has referred, you must have wondered how it was possible for one man to represent so many houses, and to give individual attention to each. Well, I have done that. And if there is any praise, you have amply bestowed it this evening. I do work very hard. I put the whole of my energy in my work, and I can assure you that with a little encouragement from you, and with a little kind indulgence, you will find that I sha'l still continue to do my duty. I have chosen difficult countries to work in; so much so, that you will find very few Englishmen that represent houses in the parts that I go to. But I must say that I have been placed in a somewhat better position than many of my fellow comrades at arms, inasmuch as I speak the languages necessary for the countries I visit. I am afraid that I am taking up too much of your time (No, no), but I should like to say one or two words. I was talking to Mr. Worthington, the gentleman who was sent by the Board of Trade of Liverpool to South America to enquire into the business that is done in that part of the world, and he agreed with me that we do not send out properly equipped men to represent this country. You know that the back-bone of this country is commerce. Here we are all sitting down and enjoying our dinner this evening, I am sure I have enjoyed mine, and I can assure you that if commerce were not prospering in your city offices, your heart would be too full to come here to feast; and I say to you that a commercial traveller going to South America and other countries, where foreign languages are a necessity, had better stay at home if he does not speak those languages. I would now like to say one or two words about the countries into which I have carried your different banners, samples, sample boxes, price lists, &c. The continent of South America is a difficult one for any Englishman to work in, inasmuch as the neighbouring States are always disagreeing, and their quarrels, which might be settled otherwise than by warfare, do much harm, and commerce in no wise improves in consequence, and besides which the customs, laws, and regulations being so changeable it is quite impossible for the supplier and buyer to know how they stand. I say to you that there is plenty of money in South America, plenty of riches, but I am afraid the Custom House tariffs are used to fill the coffers of the Treasury for political ends; thus making impossible, very often, the entry of foreign goods, by this I mean also goods of English make, into these countries. The next part of the programme on tour is the West Indian Islands, and you will agree with me if I say that it is pleasant to execute the orders that come from these parts of the world. They know how to do their business. I have very great pleasure in seeing this evening that Mr. Johnson, of Messrs. Gillespie Bros., that very esteemed house, is present here to-night, I assure you that if any of you paid a visit to the West Indian Islands you would be as heartily welcomed as your wares are. Well, gentlemen, I want your further support. I have been making a plan which I think will receive your very hearty support. This is to open a branch office in Barbados, and to live there for two years, and to work your business and to exploit it with very little extra cost to those I represent. I find that my journeys, on account of the difficulties of getting about, are by no means easy work, as I have to fly from one place to another, and to do the work in the little time I have to the best of my ability, and I think my duties are getting a little bit more onerous day by day, and although I am equal to it, I want to place my work on a sounder basis, and to open up business in the West Indies, followed (if the bubble does not burst) by an office in South America. A question that must touch the heart of every Englishman is the very sad state that the West Indies are placed in at the present time on account of the small price of their principal product, namely, sugar; and that is the reason that business in these parts has not been what I should have liked to have seen. Well I think England can be trusted to settle this matter. She can do so without getting into any trouble whatever. Mr. Chamberlain has done his best; I think there has been no unity in the matter, and I sincerely trust that for the sake of the West Indies where our flag flies, Englishmen as a whole will do their utmost to help the West Indies over the present commercial crisis. The sugar bounties cannot long stand their burden. It is all very well to give £7 or £8 as a bounty for growing sugar, but Continental governments will see the folly of their action sooner than is expected. I can assure you that England can never lose her prestige by giving help to these Islands, which want her support very badly. It is well known that Jamaica presented this country with one million sovereigns, which she has never asked to be returned, and a handsome present was made by Barbados to the home country, and she, until this present crisis came about, has never asked its return. So if we open our pockets we shall only be returning tit for tat. I have said enough. I thank you very much for the great confidence you have placed in me, and for the way in which you have received the words of my friend Mr. Dewar. I will also couple with this the gentlemen of the Committee, and I would like specially to mention the name of Mr. Kent—who has had the onerous duties of Treasurer and Secretary, and in fact, of head cook and bottle-washer—and to thank you for the way this dinner has been conducted. The Committee have my sincere thanks, and I am sure they have yours. (Hear, hear.) Well, it is a signal honour conferred on me this evening by your presence, and I can assure you that the card which has your names upon it will be treasured by me and will adorn my walls, and will be handed to my son as an heirloom which he might well be proud of. It is an honour to be surrounded by so many eminent men, and I am proud to have at my table Sir J. Heron Maxwell, Bart., also Mr. J. H. Dalziel, M.P., and Mr. J. Lowles, M.P. If we had a peep into the diaries of these gentle-men, we should find how full up they are with their numerous appointments, and it is therefore a very great pleasure to me that they have honoured this gathering with their presence. I have nothing more to say except to assure you that anything you ask me to do on your behalf and with your confidence in me will always receive the greatest possible care and best attention, and I thank you for this signal honour which I can assure you I will not fail to convey to my clients, of whom a great many are my personal friends. I thank you from the bottom of my heart, and I assure you that the pleasure of being present this evening in company with my father must have touched his heart very much indeed, as he expected when I was a boy that I should do well, as we all know fathers think great things of their children. He has been a good parent to me, and he has given me riches in the form of a good education, and I am trying my hardest to repay him for what he has done. I assure you that my father feels this signal honour which you have conferred upon me this evening. (Cheers.)

Mr. J. LOWLES. M.P., in proposing " Commerce," said that he had no notion until the Chairman mentioned his name that he was to figure on the Toast list, but he was afraid that he could not use the stereotyped phrase of being unaccustomed to public speaking, as he was a member of Parliament. Although he could not say that he had any direct connection with Commerce, he represented a constituency of between 60,000 and 70,000 workers, and it had always been one of the objects of his life to reconcile any differences which might crop up. In his opinion Capital was most indispensable to Labour, and as an illustration he might liken labour without capital to an engine without steam. In his political experience he had twice canvassed 7,000 houses and workshops for votes amongst his constituents, and he had made himself familiar with the difficulties of labour. As a student of Commerce he was a diligent reader of Blue Books, and although these were a little dry reading, they were most interesting. He was convinced that the future of this country depended very largely upon the care we took as to our trade and commerce. He was not ashamed to say that the politics he talked in the East end of London were bread-and-butter politics, because whatever might be our views about abstract questions, those in which we took the deepest interest were politics which were mixed up with the everyday life, health, comfort, and prosperity of our people. Our imports were growing to an enormous extent, and that growth was largely due to the increase in manufactured goods, whilst there had been a growing decrease in our exports. An enormous depreciation had taken place between 1890 and '95 in both imports and exports of this country, whilst again there had been an enormous rise for some reason or other between '95 and '98, but this he thought must be due to the journeys of Mr. Martinez. (Hear, hear.) It was a natural sequence, years of famine and years of plenty. The party that was responsible for the good would of course be longest in power. If politics had anything to do with it that party that helped most materially to advance the general prosperity of the country would be in the ascendency for many years to come. But what he felt about this question was that we had got to learn a great many lessons and take leaves out of the books of our neighbours. If we came to compare our export trade with the enormous growth of the export trade of Germany, it was a very serious question for us to consider. It was the duty of every man who had the interests of his country at heart to see in what direction our efforts ought to be trained in order to bring about this general prosperity which we all desired. As he had already said, it was a remarkable fact that there had been an enormous increase in our imports. Our Colonies had enormous undeveloped virginal resources, whilst we had to depend for our livelihood mainly upon our manufactures. What more natural, then, than that we should exchange our manufactures for their raw products to the mutual benefit of both? He remembered having a fierce argument about the trade of the United States. He declared that in his opinion it was not profitable that we should spend 90 millions a year, when the United States of America only spent 30 millions a year with us. It seemed that there must be some vital loss when we pay 90 millions out and only get 30 millions back. With our Colonies we did get pound for pound, and every penny of English capital invested there brought its reward in increased demands for our manufactures. Any gentleman, who in a practical way extended our commerce created new markets, like Mr. Martinez was doing, for the good, not merely of his firms, but to the general welfare of the community at large. He laid stress upon the importance, for commercial men, of Consular reports. Twenty-five years ago the British were predominant in Brazil, whilst to-day Germany, by several good methods, had completely displaced British manufactures and had established their own. What was the remedy? Intelligent highly-trained representatives, men of personality and assiduity, like Mr. Martinez, who had been honoured by being called an "Ambassador of Commerce," were wanted. This was a very serious problem. He ventured to say that Mr. Martinez was on the way to solve the question. British trade wanted waking up, and wanted maintaining, and by following up the example of his success to plant the British flag of Commerce in places where it is not yet, but where it should be. If he might revert to the point with which he started, it was of vital importance for our Commerce to be maintained and extended. He was quite sure that public opinion was just now centred on that particular point in politics. Why did we insist upon British rights being maintained in China? Because we were doing 78 per cent. of the trade that is done between China and the rest of the world, and we could not afford to lose a single point per cent. We had seen, as Lord Kitchener said the other day, that Egypt had been made what it is to-day, because wherever the British flag flies, freedom and equal justice go with it, and he is a free man to-day who only a few years ago was still a slave. He (Lord Kitchener) said : here is a new market for British trade. Although patriotism of this kind was only second to the importance which attaches to the great military success which was the backbone of this great country, yet the markets which we had secured should be maintained and extended to every part of the world. He congratulated those present upon having a man for their guest who had rightly been called an "Ambassador of Commerce." The Commerce of this country was of the most vital importance to its prosperity, and the country was under deep gratitude to men like Mr. Martinez, who go with energy and splendid enthusiasm, which were some of his distinguished characteristics, and who plant the flag of British trade. and who introduce British goods, which were better than German, and, having got his clients, acquainted them with the quality of British manufactures. One of the causes laid down for the depreciation of our export trade was the want of attention paid to packing, and the old-fashioned ways of our English manufacturers; they would not be up to date. But if the representative only went about with his eyes open and came back full of lessons he had learnt, it was the best investment any British firm could make, and it was worth paying for. He had now great pleasure in proposing "Commerce" as a real honest and British toast, and he coupled with it the name of Mr. Arthur Kent. (Cheers.)

MR. A. B. KENT said : Mr. Chairman, and Gentlemen, I am sorry that this toast was not entrusted to better hands, as in a meeting like this I am sure there are many commercial men who could have done justice to it better than I can. But I do not think there is anyone who would be more proud to respond to the toast of "Commerce" than your humble servant. I am laboring under a difficulty that the gentleman who has just spoken has said all I wanted to say on the subject. Commerce is the backbone of this country, and about that there is very little doubt. The men who sowed the seeds of the greatest empire that has ever existed, were surely the merchant venturers of the middle ages. What has made this country so great is not a feat of arms, but it has been the energy, enterprise, and integrity of this great empire. Our Colonies, of which we are so proud, were not won at the point of the sword, or kept by the power of the sword. If you want an illustration of that you have only to look at the Spanish Colonies to-day. What are they ? Gone. Napoleon has been mentioned. He once made what he thought, perhaps, a very smart remark. He said he thought that the English were a nation of shopkeepers. He did not mean it as a compliment, but I accept it as a very high compliment. I am sorry to say that our neighbours across the Channel still adhere very considerably to the ideas of this great man. I do not think that the toast of "Commerce" would be received in France to-day in the way in which it is received in this country. Unfortunately for France, they do not honour and respect commerce as they should. They think too much of militarism. Napoleon was a great soldier, and France thinks more of the soldier than of business. If a man is successful in business in France he makes a fortune, large or small, and his son does not generally continue his father's business. The man who has made the fortune retires and becomes a *rentier*, and lives on his income. The son wishes to become an official of some kind, goes into the army or becomes a *fonctionnaire* of the Government, and he loses all individuality and initiative. In this country we are proud to continue the business of our forefathers. My greatest pride is that I am one of the fourth generation in the same business. It is feelings like these that keep up the commerce of the country. British commerce is not yet ruined, and the figures quoted by Mr. Lowles about the United States —that we pay them 90 millions and they only pay us 30 millions—I should like to put in another way ; we receive from them 90 millions and send them 30 millions of goods, for Mr. Lowles would not suggest that the difference is paid for in gold (hear, hear). The day was when it was considered in this country somewhat *infra dig.* to be connected with trade, but we do not hear people sneer, nowadays, at people who are in trade. There are a great many people who rush into trade, and find, when they get there, that it is only finance, and are then rather sorry that they went there (laughter). But trade, real trade, is, as has been said, the backbone of this country, and though we hear much of what is made in Germany, I think there is a considerable amount of prosperity in this country yet. The trade of Germany has increased enormously, but you must remember they are starting at the beginning, and we are nearly, but I hope not quite, at the top of what we can do, and we shall keep to the top rung of the ladder. We are educated to-day better than we were before. A great deal has been said about technical education, and that we are taking up. Commercial education is another matter. Germany has done wonders in commercial education, but we are told that Commercial education is only just beginning in Germany. They can teach us a great deal, and we are much too conservative. We want representatives to talk the languages of the countries they visit, and we ought to act upon their advice. That is one of the things in which the British manufacturer is a little bit behind. He has the best article to offer, but it is of no use to offer it to a man who does not know how to use it. We ought to be more up to date in putting such things as price lists into Foreign languages, and using the metric system of weights and measures. It is a marvel that English trade has kept up as it has, although we do not use this system. Commerce is rather a hardy perennial that flourishes in the free air of competition, and would not do so well in the vitiated atmosphere of ultra protection. I firmly believe that the commerce of England is not yet in a dying state. England is not

Speakers at the Banquet given to Mr. Frederick A. Martinez,

HOTEL CECIL, NOVEMBER 8th, 1898.

only the greatest commercial nation, but it is the Banker and Creditor of the world, and it is the enterprise and the integrity of the British nation that have made that. I thank you very much for drinking to the toast of "Commerce." and for honouring me in allowing me to respond to it. (Cheers.)

SIR J. HERON MAXWELL proposed the Toast of the Press, and said · Mr. Chairman and Gentlemen, it is fortunate for one who, at the last moment, is asked to propose an important toast, that that toast is one which requires no eloquence on his part. Such is the power of the Press, and the position that it has attained in the present day, that it has become common for us to call it the "Fourth Estate" in the Empire. I am old enough to remember long before the telegraph system, and all those modern improvements took place, that at a convivial and pleasant reunion of this sort we could not be honoured with the presence of a large number of the daily Press, because the number of them was so very small. But now-a-days we must be very careful what we do and what we say, because we know that our views perhaps, certainly our words, may be produced, and will be produced, sometimes in a way and in a place that we little expect it. But I think a man in the present day must be very thin-skinned if he cannot stand the honest criticisms of the Press. The Press has become a power all over the world ; no matter whether it is in war, in commerce, or in social circles. there is the press ready to represent in its best form everything that takes place, and, therefore, we need not be individually or collectively under any fear whatever, if we say and act honestly to the best of our belief. It is a curious thing, I think, to reflect when you come to see every day in the newspaper, so and so says, "Oh ! That article is a libel." I say a man should not fear, whether it be in finance, or in politics, or in commerce, his acts or his words ought to be such as to defy anything but honest criticism, and we of the present day thoroughly appreciate that a man must be very thin-skinned if he cannot stand by and defend his principles. There is no doubt that we cannot get on without the Press ; we are glad to find them in every circle, glad to welcome them, because we know that they, with intelligence—with wonderful intelligence—will, and do represent, the true interests of this country, and of every phase of society, commerce, and of life. I am not going to take up your time in making a speech, because my Toast is one that can be spoken in three words : Get up, speak up, and shut up. (Laughter.) I am not going to say more, but give you most heartily, and with every honor that we can, the toast of the Press. I give you the Press, the "Fourth Estate of this Realm," and I couple with it the name of Mr. J. H. Dalziel, M.P. (Cheers.)

MR. J. H. DALZIEL, M.P. : Mr. Chairman and Gentlemen, as you have already been informed, a change was made in our toast list this evening, and it was altered at my suggestion, because I heard that Mr. T. P. O'Connor was coming, and I would have been glad indeed if he had replied to this toast, because he is a brilliant journalist, and I am sure if he had been here he would have done more justice to it than I can possibly do. However, gentlemen, in his absence I fall into the programme as arranged, and I rise to respond to this toast. It is to me a very great satisfaction that the proposer of this toast is, as he has mentioned, a countryman of my own. The name of Sir Heron Maxwell is one that is respected and held in the highest esteem, and one that was at all times revered by the inhabitants of that county. It is an honour to me to find myself to-night, without any expectation, by the side of a gentleman who is held in such high respect. I have risen to reply to the toast of the Press, but before doing so I should like to say how much I agree with some of the sentiments that have been expressed to-night, with regard to the question of commerce abroad. Mr. Lowles does not, I am sure, expect that I will agree with him in everything he said. But there is one thing which Mr. Martinez especially emphasised with which I cordially agree. I have visited almost every point which Mr. Martinez has visited. I have visited the West Indies, Buenos Ayres and the South American Continent ; I have ridden across it, and I have visited every possible centre of population, and I do most cordially emphasise that until British Manufacturers recognise that to do commerce their representatives must speak the language of the country, it is absolutely impossible to compete

Geo Harold Kent, Esq.

Jno. L. Grossmith, Esq.

Ex Sheriff Thomas R. Dewar.

W. H. Burgess, Esq.

Eugene Alberga, Esq.

Gentlemen of the Committee of the Banquet given to Mr. Frederick N. Martinez,
HOTEL CECIL, NOVEMBER 8th, 1898.

with German and other representatives of other countries. While I was in Buenos Ayres I made it my business to enquire why it was that we were not as successful as we might be with reference to our trade there, and on every side I found the answer the same. The Germans who were doing business there sent their representatives eighteen months in advance, in order to know what the requirements were. On the other hand I found that the great majority of the representatives of British houses out there did not even understand the language, and came with the ordinary price lists, and did not know what the requirements of the population were. I believe it is the difficulty in a nutshell. He must study the idiosyncracies of the people. He must anticipate the demand, and in that way he will compete with the German in the South American counties, and in that way alone. And I believe there is a splendid opportunity in that part of the world; it is the Africa and Australia of the New World. The value of land is increasing, because there are possibilities of enormous extension, because people are settling there very fast, and, so far as this country is concerned, we are absolutely unacquainted with it, and it is my belief that we shall have an enormous boom there one day. I speak particularly of Argentina, because I am more acquainted with that part, but I might extend the application of my argument, and wherever you go you will find the representatives of German firms. Now I have risen particularly to reply to the toast of the Press. I have had some association with it as a very humble worker in the past. When I was at the age of 16 I used to write the leading articles of an eminent weekly paper. The other day I came across some of my articles, and tried to read them over, but I soon gave it up as a bad job. Well, from that time I have had the honour of being associated with the Press. I am very proud of that association, and I hope I may long continue to have the honour of calling myself a pressman. We have had many charges brought against the press, but I am very glad to say that, so far as the Press of this country is concerned, it stands higher to-day than that of any other country. We have, as every other country, papers of a lower standard. but speaking generally, our Press, compared, for instance, with that of France and throughout the world, is more powerful in this country than in any other you can possibly name. I hope the Press will continue to have that power which it has had in the past, and I am sure that that power is largely increased and largely supported by the patronage which the gentlemen round this table are in the habit of extending to it. And I thank the gentlemen here to-night for their patronage, because I am sure they will find it useful to advertise. When I see the price at which some of our papers are published I almost think that there will come a time when we will have to pay the people to read them. However, I hope that the manufacturers and the advertisers will still believe in the Press as a medium of communication with their clients. I thank you for the honour you have done the Press to-night in including it in your toast list. I often wish that Mr. Martinez had been a pressman. I can imagine the envy he would cause. I can even imagine that a decision of the Cabinet Council would have been submitted to him before the Cabinet Council had taken place. (Applause.) He would make his fortune. But we admire capacity in whatever direction we have to find it, and I am here to-night because I believe Mr. Martinez is a man second to none in his own line. I know he is a man of brains, and I do not care from what country he may come. If he has ability, and if he means to keep it, that man will get on. We admire him, and we like to see a man get on, and therefore I say to Mr. Martinez that the Press will back him up in spreading British Commerce as against the commerce of any other country. I thank you for the cordiality with which you have received this toast, and I hope that the Press may long continue to be worthy of being included in the toast list of gatherings of business men in this country. (Cheers.)

MR. G. HAROLD KENT: Gentlemen, it falls to my lot this evening to follow this rhetorical display. It is my pleasure now to rise to propose the health of our Chairman. (Hear, hear.) Gentlemen, we here are all Englishmen. We are all under the glorious flag but while we are Englishmen, there are parts of the nation whom we welcome most strongly. They are our Colonies. I would like to say that in any country that was ever colonized

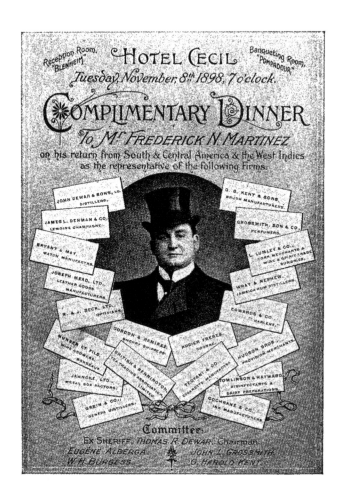

FACSIMILE OF THE MENU CARD

OF THE DINNER AT THE HOTEL CECIL, NOVEMBER 8TH, 1898,

GIVEN BY

The Chiefs of the Houses represented by Mr. Martinez.

a Scotchman was there before any other nation, and what this country owes to the Scotchman, I doubt if she will ever repay. Scotchmen were there immediately they were required. They are the finest pioneers of the Colonies of this Nation. They are magnificent specimens of humanity, and if you wish any more, you have only to look at the regiments that have gone to victory for the Queen they love. There is also another nationality that we most honor. We are all Englishmen first of all, but we have in addition to Scotchmen, Mr. Martinez, who comes from the very oldest race in the world: the Jews. We all think a very great deal of the Jews, and, Gentlemen, there is no one here to-night who will doubt what I say comes from my heart. Mr. Martinez is of that ancient and honorable Nationality. (Hear, hear.) When we find him as the guest of the evening, toasted by our Chairman who is a Scotchman, and both of them Englishmen, we may know that we have a very fine backbone to our meeting here to-night. Gentlemen, after the rhetorical display that we have had all round to-night, it is not for me to add many words, but I do want to add one, and that is, the Toast that I have the honour to propose, namely, the health of the Gentleman who is occupying the Chair this evening, the gentleman who has raised his firm to a pinnacle that all other Scotch whisky distillers envy very much. (Hear, hear.) Gentlemen, we are proud of our Guest this evening, and he has been toasted by every speaker, and we are proud of our Chairman. I now ask you to stand up, to fill your glasses, and to drink long life, health, happiness, and prosperity to Mr. Dewar. (Cheers.)

MR. DEWAR : Mr. Harold Kent and Gentlemen, after the very cordial way in which you have received me to-night, I must say that I feel somewhat nervous to inflict upon you any of my further indifferent eloquence. You have been good enough, Mr. Kent, to mix up the Nationalities in a way, and it reminds me of a remark I heard in San Francisco about four years ago. You have been very complimentary to both races, and *apropos* of that, an American friend said to me : " I guess in San Francisco we have got a funny breed, but the best man we can find here is a Yankee Jew pedlar, with a Scotch connection, and you cannot beat him." (Laughter.) I think that remark applies somewhat to your remark. You have been very flattering to the Scotch in mixing us up with those *bon financiers*. What would it be for England, France or Germany, if they had not these grand financiers ? We all know the story of that grandest of all English politicians, Disraeli ; it is very significant to-day. When he went to finance the British Nation he started the red herring on the path, in capturing almost the entire control of the Suez Canal. He interviewed in the off-season the other great financier Rothschild, and when he was leaving his office he said : " Now supposing my Cabinet will not see this investment of the four millions in the light that you and I see it, what am I do do ? " Rothschild, in a casual sort of way, said : " We will throw it into our own investments." (Laughter.) That is why I say that you have been good enough to mix us up in the way you have done. The Englishman always says that the Scotchman keeps the Sabbath and everything else he can lay his hands on. (Laughter.) We certainly try to do so, but the other races do it also. (Laughter.) And you say they are great pioneers. Well, there the other race is greater, but I believe we do trace our pedigree back a little bit, because there was an Englishman discussing this question with a Scotchman. Of course, he went back a long way, as far back as Noah, in the Book that the Scotchman would rely upon, saying that we are not mentioned, and he further said that we were not in the Ark. " Oh ! I can well account for that," was the answer, " because the McGregors had a boat of their own." (Laughter.) Well, gentlemen, I think you have had sufficient Scotch this evening. I thank you very much for the very kind reception which you have given me to-night, and we have to thank our friend Mr. Martinez for bringing together such a consensus of power as we have got around us. I thank you for the very great honour you have done me in putting me in this Chair, to sit and listen to such eloquent speeches as we have heard to-night, and in saying that, I am sure that you do not wish to have any further of my indifferent eloquence, and I will simply say that I thank you most sincerely. (Cheers.)

INCIDENTS ON

Mr Frederick N. Martinez's Journeys

AT HOME AND ABROAD.

MR. FREDERICK N. MARTINEZ

ON THE

WEST INDIAN QUESTION.

Reproduced from **The Sun**, *London Evening Paper*,
Monday, December 5th, 1898.

"A BEGGARLY LOAN."

TO THE EDITOR OF "THE SUN."

I read in your leader of Saturday, December 3rd, your very plain, outspoken remarks on the scheme which has just been made known for the relief of the West Indies. I can assure you that the beggarly contribution of the Home Government to these islands cannot but be received by them with some amount of surprise and disfavour.

Is this all that is going to be done after all the talk that has taken place, and after the visit of the Governor of Barbados to this country? What is the good of it? Does the Government take into consideration that Barbados, for its size, is the most thickly populated place in the world? What good is this small grant to them, and what are they going to do after this paltry allowance has been expended?

I quite agree with you when you say, "And this is the practical outcome of the 'Imperialist idea' which animates us all nowadays."

I speak with some amount of knowledge on this question, representing in the West Indies twenty-five of the most important houses in every branch of trade in this country, and I must say that the insignificant grant and beggarly loan of our Government to Barbados and St. Vincent is of no use whatever to them to cope with their present difficulties and troubles.

The Government is by no means doing its duty to its West Indian possessions.

FREDERICK N. MARTINEZ.

117 ELGIN AVENUE, MAIDA VALE,
LONDON, W.

December 3rd, 1898.

⁘ Extracts from the Press ⁘

AT HOME AND ABROAD.

Commerce says, " A commercial among commercials, Mr. MARTINEZ is a man well worth knowing, and although only a young man, we should say knows more of the conditions under which British manufactures are marketed abroad than anyone else I have come across, in the course of a pretty wide acquaintance with travellers."

The *Commercial Traveller* says, "Mr. MARTINEZ is modest, you would not think it. Has he not at 26 been everywhere, seen everybody, hobnobbed with governors and rulers galore, put consuls right, suggested the proper politics and commercial methods to foreign lands, enlightened the Press everywhere, and presided over sweepstakes on board ship ? "

The *Tribune of Barbados* says, "We have much pleasure in welcoming to our island a well known business traveller in the person of Mr. F. N. MARTINEZ, who is making a tour in the West Indian Islands, South and Central America. We wish him the success he richly deserves, and the liberal support of all Barbadians."

The *Daily Chronicle*, British Guiana, says, "Mr. FREDERICK N. MARTINEZ has arrived in the colony, representing several important commercial houses. We may mention that Mr. Martinez was a delegate at the Antwerp Exhibition, where he succeeded in obtaining for the firms that he represented there the highest possible awards, besides receiving for himself the conspicuous recognition of His Majesty King Leopold of the Belgians, as well as the delegates of the French Republic, and the Turkish Empire."

The *Star and Herald*, Panama, says, "Among the passengers arrived at Colon per Royal Mail S.S. " Don," is Mr. F. N. MARTINEZ. Our young friend, who has visited the principal centres of population in Africa, as well as in Europe, in connection with the great establishments he represents, lived for some years on the Isthmus. We feel sure that with a thorough knowledge of the Spanish language coupled with a genial and pleasant disposition, very necessary qualifications, and highly indispensable for one in his position, we feel certain that he will meet with much success."

The *Gleaner of Jamaica* says, "We understand that Mr. F. N. MARTINEZ is in our midst ; he represents some important houses, which we can only add do him very great credit."

The *European Mail* says, " We hear that Mr. F. N. MARTINEZ goes out in the R. M. S. " Orinoco," for a tour in the West Indian Islands and the South and Central American Republics, in the interest of the well-known firm of Messrs. John Dewar & Sons, of Perth and London."

The *Sussex Evening News* says, " Mr. MARTINEZ is one of those persons who is more of a Quaker in the matter of speech, and it is surprising how the Han-Chairman found out all about his being interested in Johnny Dewar's Whiskys, Lemoine Champagne, Hudson Brothers' Provisions, etc., etc., etc. We regret to find our friend was not riding in his Bath chair for pleasure, but as the result of an accident, not from bicycle riding, but trying to put in four days' work in an hour, in the interests of the large army of firms he represents."

The *Stock Exchange* says, " Mr. MARTINEZ, who is a very young man for the amount of work he has done, and the high place he has won for himself in business circles, both in England and on the Continent, is the master of many languages."

The *Barbados Advocate* says, "There are few commercial travellers better known to the West Indies than Mr. F. N. MARTINEZ; he is always to be found up to his ears in work. Mr. MARTINEZ, who has been styled a 'commercial among commercials,' is not only a keen business man, but a traveller well acquainted with Cuba, South and Central America, and the West Indies."

Gall's News Letter, of Jamaica, says, "Mr. F. N. MARTINEZ, the irrepressible mass of volubility, has once more besieged this island. Mr. MARTINEZ is energy personified, and looms very largely upon the commercial horizon, not only in his person, but in his resistless power of obtaining orders. Mr. MARTINEZ is the valuable agent of many of the foremost European houses, whose goods abound in these Islands."

The *Colon Telegram* says, "A well known business man is amongst us. Mr. MARTINEZ has again arrived on the Isthmus, he knows he is welcome, and we look forward with much pleasure to his periodical visits."

The *Chilian Times* says, "The king of commercials and everybody's friend has just arrived from England, via the Straits of Magellan. Mr. MARTINEZ is literally weighed down with orders : he is a splendid fellow and deserving of unlimited patronage. Mr. MARTINEZ looks remarkably well, and as jolly as ever."

The *Belgian News* says, "We wish MARTINEZ, who is well known in Antwerp and Belgium, the same success as he has lately had in South America and the West Indies, and we feel sure that with his easy manner and knowledge of the French tongue, that Brussels will heartily welcome him."

The *Colonies and India* says, "Many appreciative notices have lately appeared in the West Indian press concerning Mr. F. N. MARTINEZ, the enterprising traveller, who returned the other day from a business tour through the West Indian Islands, and the South and Central American Republics. The popularity of Mr. MARTINEZ in those parts of the world is only exceeded by John Dewar & Sons' Whisky itself, which is saying something."

The *Port of Spain Gazette*, Trinidad, says, "We have again the pleasure of welcoming to the "Land of the Humming Bird" the popular of popular travellers, Mr. F. N. MARTINEZ. We have no hesitation in saying that Mr. MARTINEZ does a very fine business here, and we have not the least doubt that he will continue to do so.

The London *Sportsman* says, "Mr. MARTINEZ is a smart man of business, a capital whip, a linguist of no mean abilities, and a diplomatist, qualifications which eminently fit him for responsible representative duties."

The *Jamaica Post* says, "THE ARRIVAL OF A NOTED COMMERCIAL TRAVELLER.—The arrival of Mr. F. N. MARTINEZ, one of the heroes of Messrs. John Dewar & Sons, will be noted with pleasure by his many Jamaican friends. Mr. Sam Collier, of Rylands, has been considered the "doyen" of com mercial travellers in the West Indies, but he has now retired with a pension, and holding shares in nearly every paying company on the face of the earth. Mr. MARTINEZ follows in his wake, and those who know him say that Mr. FREDERICK N. MARTINEZ is the Archangel who can roll up Sam Collier in a snuff box any day he pleases to do so."

The *Malta Chronicle* says, "Mr. MARTINEZ, though a very young man, has an income, from a rapidly increasing business, all over the world, and I will guarantee that no merchant in Malta works out with the labour of his hands a larger nett result."

Freir's Colonial and Foreign Register says "THE PRINCE OF COMMERCIAL AMBASSADORS.—Mr. FREDERICK N. MARTINEZ is one of the most remarkable young men we ever met, and in a career embracing a long course of travel, is the embodiment of good humour and ready wit, and it is easily understood why he is so uniformly successful in his long and wide-spread journeys throughout the world."

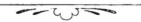

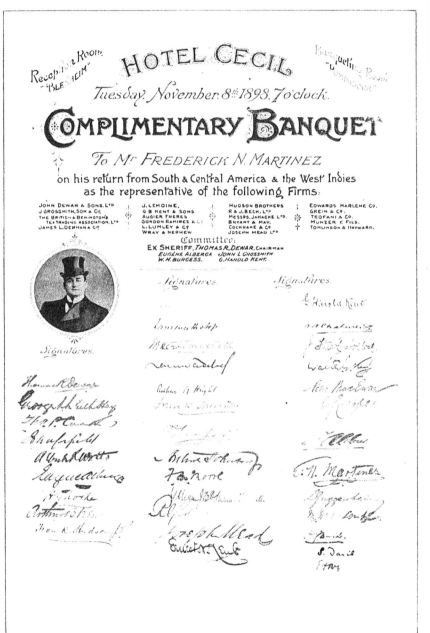

Signatures of some of the Guests present at the Banquet

GIVEN TO

Mr. MARTINEZ at the Hotel Cecil, November 8th, 1898.

A feW Press Comments

On the recent Complimentary Banquet (Hotel Cecil, London),
given in honour of Mr. FREDERICK N. MARTINEZ
by the Heads of the Houses he represents.

———— ✦ ————

THE PELICAN.
London, November 19th, 1898.

"A very interesting dinner was given last week at the Hotel Cecil, in honour of Mr. Frederick N. Martinez, a gentleman whose commercial exploits in various portions of the world are of a distinguished character. Mr. ex-Sheriff Thomas Dewar filled the chair, and amused everyone by his clever and humorous speech. Mr. Lowles, M.P., also spoke well, and Mr. G. Harold ⟨ent showed that he is a clever orator, as well as a smart business man.

"Among those who supported Mr. Martinez were Sir Heron Maxwell, Bart., Mr. Dalziel, M.P., Mr. G. Leith Hay, Mr. Bancroft of Barbados, Mr. Johnson (of the well-known firm, Messrs. Gillespie Brothers), Mr. Walter ⟨ent, Mr. Eugene Alberga, Mr. John L. Grossmith, Mr. Frank Hudson, Mr. Teofani, Mr. E. N. Martinez, Mr. R. G. Edwards, Mr. F. Aldous, Mr. P. McEwan, and many others. Mr. Martinez made a capital speech, and then the photographic artist caused a miniature explosion, which filled the room with fog and caused every one to blink."

————

THE MORNING ADVERTISER.
London, Wednesday, November 9th, 1898.

"DINNER TO MR. F. N. MARTINEZ.

"Mr. F. N. Martinez was last night entertained at dinner at the Hotel Cecil by the representatives of several well-known firms, amongst whom were John Dewar and Sons, Bryant and May, Gordon, Ramirez and Co., L. Lumley and Co., John Grossmith and Son, and G. B. ⟨ent and Sons. Mr. Martinez has just returned from a journey to the West Indies and Central and South America, and it was thought that it would be a delicate compliment to that gentleman, and at the same time a pleasant way of celebrating his return for the firms he had represented with so much success, to give him the opportunity of meeting all his friends together. Mr. T. R. Dewar presided, and was supported by Sir Heron Maxwell, Mr. J. Lowles, M.P., Mr. J. Dalziel, M.P., Mr. Arthur Johnson, Mr. E. N. Martinez, Mr. J. L. Grossmith, Mr. G. Harold ⟨ent, M. E. Alberga, Mr. W. H. Burgess, Mr. Teofani, Mr. F. Aldous, and others.

"After the loyal toasts,

"The Chairman stated that it then became his privilege to ask them to drink to the toast of the evening, 'Our Guest.' Theirs, he remarked, was a unique gathering in honour of a unique man, inasmuch as he alone represented so many firms, each of whom owned to being second to none in the United ⟨ingdom. (Hear, hear.) Mr. Martinez, he considered, must have been reared in a very extraordinary manner—perhaps like Romulus and Remus—because he had developed extraordinary ability. (Hear, hear, and laughter.) They had to thank him for the marvellous way in which he had represented them one and all in various parts of the world, and he had the assurance of every principal there that they were glad to welcome him back from the unsavory countries, famed for yellow jack and typhoid, which he had visited. (Hear, hear.) They all looked upon him as their indefatigable and irresistible ambassador of commerce. (Hear, hear.) He ventured to believe that Mr. Martinez was but just beginning his career, and would yet further surprise them all, and he wished him good health and long life to serve them in the future as he had done in the past. (Hear, hear.)

"Mr. Martinez, who was given a most cordial reception, having thanked them for the kindly greeting they had extended to him, referred to the present condition of the West Indies, remarking that he firmly believed that England might be trusted to deal fairly and wisely with that matter. She could do so without getting into trouble, but although Mr. Chamberlain had done his best, there still was a lack of unity on the question. He could assure them that

England would lose no prestige by giving help to those islands. (Hear, hear.) He might remind them that about the middle of the present century Jamaica had given England a million sterling which had never yet been demanded back; so that if they were to open their pockets they would but be giving tit for tat. (Hear, hear.) Mr. Martinez concluded by thanking them for the kind confidence they had placed in him, and for the cordial manner in which they had welcomed him back to England. (Hear, hear.)

"Mr. J. Lowles, M.P., then submitted 'Commerce,' to which Mr. Arthur B. Kent responded, both gentlemen urging the advisability of commercial firms, when dealing with fareign countries, adopting the metric system, presenting price lists printed in the language of the country, employing representatives who spoke the language of the country, and supplying goods the country needed, not only goods they manufactured."

COMMERCE.
London, November 16th, 1898.

"'Commerce' long ago claimed kinship in interview form with Mr Frederick N. Martinez. Linguist, plausible, full of tact and ready wit, this ambassador of commerce goes everywhere the globe around, and in many countries has he booked orders for various kinds of goods. Now he will be selling cigarettes and dry champagne to the magnates of a South American Republic; anon he is discussing the sugar question with the planters of his native isle, St. Thomas; a fortnight later he is found disposing of brushes and tinned provisions in feverish West Coast towns. Occasionally he comes home for a brief spell from one of his long journeys. Mr. Martinez is just now in England, and on the 8th inst. the heads of the firms he represents entertained him to a complimentary banquet, when the guest of the evening and others made speeches which were in accordance with the occasion that had called them together."

THE HOTEL.
London, November, 1898.
"A CHAMPION OF COMMERCE.
"MR. FREDERICK N. MARTINEZ.

"On the evening of Tuesday, the 8th inst., one of the most interesting trade gatherings that has been held in London for a considerable time took place. We refer to the complimentary dinner given on that date at the Hotel Cecil, to celebrate the return from the West Indies and Central and South America of Mr. Frederick N. Martinez, a gentleman who has won for himself a higher place in business circles, probably, than any other man on the road. Mr. Martinez may, indeed, be unhesitatingly termed the Prince of Commercial Ambassadors, and, considering his age, his achievements are nothing short of marvellous. He was born in St. Thomas but twenty-six years ago, yet there is hardly a place in the civilised world that he has not visited, and he must have circled the globe half a dozen times at least. What is even more worthy of note, he has everywhere made hosts of friends, and opened up fresh markets for British trade, the number of which is positively astonishing. At the outset of his travelling career, in fact, he resolved to work countries which Englishmen had hitherto found it extremely difficult to work, and he has pursued this intention in every place he has visited, until his labours were attended with the results he desired.

"Of course, this involved an enormous amount of labour and perseverance, but Mr. Martinez's stock of energy is illimitable, and he has never left a stone unturned that was calculated to enable him fairly to achieve his end. Languages and dialects he has studied by the dozen, and he has learnt more, perhaps, about the commercial methods of the places he has visited than any man alive. He could give points to the Board of Trade, and the individual who could tell him anything he does not know about sugar would be hard to find.

"Perhaps the greatest of his qualifications as a commercial traveller, however, is that he thoroughly understands the character of the people resident in the countries he works. His invariable geniality, his great powers of conversation, his 'pretty wit'—to borrow a phrase from our forefathers—and his straighforwardness, secure him a ready passport to the esteem of everybody he meets, and like a true ambassador of commerce he not only keeps his eyes persistently open to, but respects, the weaknesses and foibles of men. No man, moreover, appreciates more fully the value of the Press to a business traveller, and one of the most interesting incidents of his numerous journeyings was a dinner he gave to a large number of leading West India journalists. His ability as a business man amount, in a word, to genius.

"The complimentary dinner to which we referred at the beginning of the present article was but a fitting compliment to such a man, and we regret that pressure on our space prevents us from giving more than the following brief report of the banquet. It was given by several of the firms which Mr. Martinez represents, amongst them being John Dewar and Sons, Bryant and May, Gordon, Ramirez and Co., L. Lumley and Co., John Grossmith and Son, and G. B. Kent and Sons ; and the arrangements were carried out by a committee, including Mr. ex-Sheriff Thomas R. Dewar (who presided). Mr. Eugene Alberga, Mr. W. H. Burgess, Mr. John L. Grossmith, and Mr. G. Harold Kent, who were supported at the dinner by Sir Heron Maxwell, Bart., Mr. T. P. O'Connor, M.P., Mr. Arthur Johnson, Mr. E. N Martinez (father of the guest), Mr. F. Moore, Mr. J. Lowles, M.P., Mr. J. Dalziel, M.P., Mr. Teofani, Mr. F. Aldous, and a host of other shining lights in the business world."

THE WINE TRADE REVIEW.
London, November 15th, 1898.

"There was an interesting gathering at the Hotel Cecil, W.C., on the 8th inst., when Mr. Frederick N. Martinez was entertained at a complimentary dinner by a number of firms, on whose behalf he has been travelling in the West Indies and Central and South America. Mr. T. R. Dewar, J.P., D.L., presided, and was supported by members of all the other firms concerned, as well as by a number of friends. The proceedings throughout were of a most cordial character, and the reception given to Mr. Martinez should serve as a stimulus to other representatives of commercial houses."

THE LICENSING WORLD AND LICENSED TRADE REVIEW.
London, November 12th, 1898.
"DINNER TO MR. F. N. MARTINEZ.

"Mr. F. N. Martinez, who has just returned from a business trip to the West Indies and Central and South America, was on Tuesday night entertained at a complimentary dinner at the Hotel Cecil by the representatives of several well-known firms, amongst whom were : John Dewar and Sons, Bryant and May, Gordon, Ramirez and Co., J. Lumley and Co., John Grossmith and Son, and G. B. Kent and Sons. Mr. T. R. Dewar, who presided, was supported by Sir Heron Maxwell, Mr. J. Lowles, M.P., Mr. Dalziel, M.P., Mr. Arthur Johnson, Mr. E. N. Martinez, Mr. J. L. Grossmith, Mr. G. Harold Kent, Mr. E. Alberga, Mr. W. H. Burgess, Mr. Teofani, Mr. F. Aldous, and others.

"After the loyal toasts,

"The Chairman stated that it was his privilege to ask them to drink to the toast of the evening, 'Our Guest.' Theirs, he remarked, was a unique gathering in honour of a unique man, inasmuch as he alone represented so many firms, each of whom claimed to be second to none in the United Kingdom. (Hear, hear.) They had to thank Mr. Martinez for the marvellous way in which he had represented them one and all in various parts of the world, and he had the assurance of every principal there that they were glad to welcome him back from the unsavory countries, famed for yellow jack and typhoid, which he had visited. (Hear, hear.) They all looked upon him as their indefatigable and irresistible ambassador of commerce. (Hear, hear.) He ventured to believe that Mr. Martinez was but just beginning his career, and would yet further surprise them all, and he wished him good health and long life to serve them in the future as he had done in the past. (Hear, hear.)

"Mr. Martinez, who was given a most cordial reception, related his experiences, and concluded by thanking them for the confidence they had placed in him, and for the cordial manner in which they had welcomed him back to England. (Hear, hear.)

"Other toasts followed."

THE COMMERCIAL TRAVELLER AND RAILWAY AND HOTEL JOURNAL.
London, November 19th, 1898.

"Mr. F. N. Martinez, a sketch of whose career appeared in a recent issue of *The Commercial Traveller*, has had further honours thrust upon him. In company with many others, I was present the other evening at a banquet at the Hotel Cecil given to him as a compliment on his return from abroad. I cannot repeat one half of the many good things said on his behalf; but as all the firms whom he represents contributed to the banquet, and there were present, in addition, such M.P.'s as Messrs J. Dalziel, J. Lowles, and T. P. O'Connor, one can imagine how well a colonial traveller is received after his long journeys. A brief report of the proceedings appears in another column."

THE CHEMIST AND DRUGGIST.
London, November 12th, 1898.

"ON Tuesday evening, Mr. F. N. Martinez, who has just returned from South and Central America and West Indies, as the representative of a score of firms whose cards surrounded his portrait on the menu card, was entertained by his principals to dinner at the Hotel Cecil. The company included Sir J. Heron Maxwell, Bart., Mr. J. Lowles, M.P., and Mr. J. H. Dalziel, M.P., and was presided over by Mr. T. R. Dewar, ex-Sheriff of London. Mr. J. L. Grossmith (J. Grossmith & Son, Newgate Street), and Mr. J. Harold Kent (G. B. Kent & Sons) occupied the Vice-Chairs. As the Chairman remarked, in proposing the health of the guest of the evening, it was an unique gathering for an unique man, and he spoke of Mr. Martinez's remarkable success in pushing trade in the Western hemisphere during the past three years. Mr. Martinez, in his reply, mentioned that Mr. Worthington, who went out to South America to investigate the markets there on behalf of the Board of Trade, had told him that ignorance of Spanish on the part of English travellers in South America was one of the chief reasons why British firms did not make the progress there that continental firms do. He also referred to the great future there is for trade in the West Indies, and mentioned that it is his intention to reside during the next two years in Barbados, in order to further the interests of the firms he represents. He believes the trade of the West Indies ought to be equal to that of South America or Australia, as the population is greater, and with encouragement from the home Government the trade should develop enormously. Following the excellent yet modest speech from Mr. Martinez, came a series of orations from other invited guests. Mr. Lowles, M.P., in giving the toast of 'Commerce,' referred to the encroachment upon British trade by Germans, and regretted that our imports from the United States were £90,000,000 a year, and our exports to that country only £30,000,000. He thought that it should be the other way about. Mr. Arthur B. Kent, in responding to the toast, questioned the soundness of Mr. Lowles' logic, saying that it was not bad for us that we could get £90,000,000 worth of American goods for £30,000,000 of our own manufactures. Independent of that, Mr. Kent's speech showed a firm grasp of the directions in which British trade has suffered or is developing, and he stated plainly that there is no fear for the future if business men who have done well keep their sons at the business. Sir. J. Heron Maxwell toasted 'The Press,' to which Mr. J. H. Dalziel, M.P., replied in a plea for greater attention by British houses to South American markets.

"It was eleven before the company separated, and all expressed high pleasure at the pleasant and profitable nature of the evening."

THE JEWISH CHRONICLE.
London, November 11th, 1898.

"Last Tuesday evening, at the Hotel Cecil, Mr. F. N. Martinez was entertained at dinner by the heads of many firms of which he is the representative. The occasion was unique in so far as it was perhaps the first time that such a method had been adopted by the chiefs of business houses to emphasize their recognition of the success of one of their ambassadors of commerce. Mr. F. N. Martinez is a pioneer of the system of commercial travelling, which foreign competition of late years is just bringing into vogue, amongst English firms sending their representatives on business intent to various parts of the world, instead of many printed circulars and price lists.

" Mr. ex-Sheriff Thomas R. Dewar presided at the dinner. In proposing the toast of the guest of the evening he spoke in highly laudatory terms of Mr. Martinez's commercial ability, smartness and integrity; and Mr. J. Lowles, M.P., in proposing the toast of ' Commerce,' commented upon the importance of the methods in which Mr. Martinez had successfully been the pioneer in developing fields of British Trade, and even recovering ground that had been lost through foreign competition.

" Mr. F. Martinez expressed his keen appreciation of the signal honour that had been shown him on that occasion, and also spoke on other matters of great interest to the firms he represented."

TABLE TALK.
London, November 12th, 1898.
(*Which gives a reproduction of the Menu Card.*)

" An Ambassador of Commerce—Mr. Frederick N. Martinez—was fêted at the Hotel Cecil at a gathering probably unique, the occasion being the delight to honour as their representative in South and Central America this gentleman. To do one thing well is enough for most people, but here was a guest who by the unanimous testimony of those directly interested, was able to do twenty and more. One can only exclaim with the Dominie, ' Prodigious!' Equally remarkable is the large field Mr. Martinez covers. Brazil, or Argentine, or Bolivia, would afford range enough for most active men, especially with such a pack of firms to represent But here is a gentleman whose ample embrace includes the whole of South America, and who takes up the West Indies as a make-weight. ' Prodigious!'

" The Chairman of the evening, Mr. ex-Sheriff Dewar, would not have been the humorous man he is, if he had passed some openings for fun presented by the many-sided guest of the evening. But when he called Mr. Martinez an Ambassador of Commerce, and insisted that the present and future welfare of the country was bound up with commerce, he struck a deeper note—one that appealed immediately to his audience, and one that was not suffered to remain silent during the remainder of the evening. Mr. Lowles, M.P., Mr. J. H. Dalziel, M.P., and Sir Heron Maxwell, Bart., were among the speakers, and all of them stated that the commercial supremacy of this country should be maintained and the value of such men as Mr. Martinez for the work.

" Mr. Lowles, M.P., whose capacity for Blue Books and other departmental monstrosities excited the ungrudging admiration of his audience, said it was the imperative necessity of English trade that they should be represented by men who would take the trouble to understand the people and their needs. In this respect especially we had hitherto been obstinate in our efforts. With the suave Mr. Martinez as guest, it was obvious to pass from the general to the particular, and to speak in the first place of his linguistic knowledge, and in the next of his wonderful use of that knowledge."

THE MINERAL WATER RECORDER.
London, November 8th, 1898.

" We have much pleasure in presenting our readers with a portrait of Mr. Frederick N. Martinez—a gentleman who has done as much, perhaps, to promote the commercial welfare of this country as anyone. Mr. Martinez has, indeed, been very justly called the prince of commercial travellers, and there are many quarters of the globe in which British productions would probably never have been known, far less extensively used, but for the strenuous efforts he has put forth to secure a market for them. In Central and South America, in particular, he has done wonders for English traders, and the dinner given him on his recent return from those countries by several of the firms whom he represents was but a fitting reward for his labours on their behalf."

Reprinted from .
SELL'S COMMERCIAL INTELLIGENCE.
London, Saturday, December 17th, 1898.

" No subject is more frequently commended to the attention of the British trader by our Consuls abroad than the employment of travellers who understand the customs and languages of the countries they have to visit. Over and over again it is pointed out that the trade of Great Britain suffers through sending abroad not only price lists printed in English, but agents who are guiltless of any acquaintance with foreign languages. A representative of *Commercial Intelligence* has had the pleasure of a talk with Mr. F. N. Martinez, a commercial representative whose qualifications should satisfy the most exacting critic. Gifted with an irresistible geniality and a flow of language calculated to worm an order out of the most stony-hearted buyer, it is not to be wondered at that over a score of leading British firms have entrusted their interests in the West Indies in his hands. Mr. Martinez is naturally interested in the fate of the islands where he was born, and with which he is so intimately acquainted.

"'How often is it remembered,' he said, 'that a century ago Jamaica gave the mother country a million sterling in her hour of need, and that unlucky Barbados also contributed handsomely at a time when England badly wanted it? Now the unfortunate planters are in no position to give. They are heavily in debt, and their industry ruined by British fiscal policy which, whatever its effects at home, inflicts great hardship upon them. Surely Great Britain cannot now refuse her assistance.'

"'Do you consider, Mr. Martinez, that the planters have shown lack of enterprise, and that their misfortunes are their own fault?'

"'Certainly not. It is easy to talk of replacing sugar by other industries; but it must be remembered that this cannot be done in one year or two years, and sometimes, indeed, it cannot be done at all. The soil of Barbados, as you pointed out in your last issue, is only suitable for the growth of the sugar cane. Doubtless much could be done in Barbados by the establishment of central factories and introduction of fresh capital; but, as I said before, it is a matter of time, and the only immediate remedy I know of is the simple one of fighting the continental sugar bounties. There is another point I should like to mention in connection with the West Indies, and it is with regard to Jamaica rum. It is almost impossible for Jamaica to export rum to England, owing to the filthy trash which is sent over here from Hamburg at a price Jamaica cannot compete with.'

"'You are, of course, acquainted with Cuba, Mr. Martinez. Do you think that the new *régime* will give the British trader a better opening?'

"'Certainly not, at present. Quite apart from the question of how America will arrange the tariff, you must bear in mind that the Cubans are not yet reconciled to the American yoke. It is true they do not love Spain, but neither do they love the Yankee. The same is true of the Philippines. The Americans have a difficult task before them; rebellions in the near future are probable, and years will probably elapse before any material improvement will take place.'

"'And what of South America, which you know so well?'

"'I can bear out much that Mr. Worthington says in the reports you have published. It is certainly the case that the majority of British firms do not recognise the necessity of sending abroad qualified travellers and properly-translated catalogues. I have known of cases where price lists have been used by cute German travellers to note prices and go one lower. Then, of course, there is practically no protection for the English manufacturers' trade marks and registered labels. They are copied wholesale. I know an American firm who will supply you with exact fac-similes of the cases, capsules, labels, bottles, envelopes, corks etc., that distinguish any well-known brand of champagne or other liquor, at the low price of one dollar per case. In the same way I have known good brands of whisky copied in the most unblushing way, and filthy German stuff sent to our Colonies and foreign countries in bottles labelled and got up in imitation of British goods. It is difficult, of course, to deal with such competition as this.'

"'Is it your opinion that the British trader is not keeping pace with his American and German rivals?'

"'I keep my eyes open, and have unfortunately to confess to myself that American tools, for instance, find more favour with foreign buyers than British, and that great inroads on the Manchester trade have been made by the Germans and French, who succeed in turning out an article that is cheaper and more attractive to the foreign buyer.'

" Finally, Mr. Martinez was good enough to express his warm admiration of our efforts to popularise commercial intelligence. 'For one,' said he, 'who reads a Blue Book, thousands read your paper. You are doing a great service.'"

Lightning Source UK Ltd.
Milton Keynes UK
UKHW02f2032260318
320074UK00023B/1094/P

9 781333 347383